I-Lan' in di Sun

Nana Farika Berhane

Nana Farika Berhane
April 8, 2015
Ancestral guidance +
Protection

Cover design by Marcus Garvey Burrowes.

Layout design by Susan Lee Quee.

Livication

To my ancestral blood family and cultural women in my island who provided guidance in my journey towards cultural integrity especially to the spirit of Grandi Nanni, Mrs. Amy Jacques Garvey, and Louise Bennett. Miss Lou, ah luv yu fi true.

Give Thanks

To the Creator for giving me the health, strength and inspiration to complete writing this book.

Special thanks to all those who assisted on my journey towards writing and publishing this book, which encompassed Kingston, the Blue Mountains and wider Jamaica, California, New York, Washington DC, and Addis Ababa, Ethiopia. Give thanks to my son Dr. Ashay for providing support and technical/editorial/production skills while I worked on the manuscript, my son Marcus for designing the book cover, my daughter Sahai for insightful critiques and suggestions about the poems, Ras Iley for being like a son to me during the bitter winter of 2013/2014 while I was working on completing the book, to Claudette Henry and Sister Nadia Mahmud for typing assistance, and Susan Lee Quee for her patience with our layout changes.

Contents

Preface

There was a cultural revolution in Jamaica and throughout the Caribbean during the 1970's expressed by Rastafari and the philosophy, lifestyle and music/art they developed and inspired. An essential aspect of this revolution was literary expression and experiment and at the heart of this was Farika Berhane, then developing out of her more middle-class Norma Hamilton, journalist, nativist, scholar, researcher, worker and creative writer.

Professor Kamau Brathwaite,
Distinguished poet and historian,
Professor Emeritus of Comparative Literature,
New York University.

Introduction

The idea of an earthly paradise is no mere metaphor of a creative imagination. It is a term that literally describes the tropical beauty of the Caribbean Islands with a daily temperature usually between 80-85 degrees Fahrenheit accompanied by a cool breeze and a breathtaking landscape. For Farika Berhane, this island beauty was mirrored in a childhood of songs, games, stories, abundant nurturing and wonderment told in a language familiar and musical: Jamaican patois.

Louise Bennett brought to Jamaican poetry what Paul Laurence Dunbar brought to African-American poetry. She wrote in the folk dialect of Jamaica, making us realize that the language itself was poetry possessing the idioms and imagery of a rich folk culture and the musical rhythms of a calypso sea. *I-Lan' in di Sun* is an invocation of memory; childhood memories, memories of young love, marriage, history, revolutions and of a beloved country left behind for a new life in the United States. Inspired by Louise Bennett, Nana Farika writes in the language she remembers hearing while growing up.

The book opens with poems in honor of the legendary Maroons who, under the leadership of Captain

Kojo, successfully fought the British army until they were forced to negotiate a peace treaty acknowledging Maroon freedom. A proud descendant of the Maroons, Nana Farika brings a Maroon and Rastafarian sensibility and world view to her poetry. The *Nanni* poems in honor of the legacy of National Hero Nanny (Nanni) of the Maroons set the tone and timbre of the collection that traces a rites of passage trajectory of Nana Berhane's life from birth to puberty, to adulthood and marriage, all of which culminate in a deep commitment to Pan-African liberation. Nana, who is also a journalist, playwright, storyteller and educator, is no armchair scholar/poet. A woman of her word, she is a poet that lives and breathes her words of revolutionary action, but it is the revolutionary action of a wise woman rooted in the spiritual culture of Rastafari. Thus, her love for her people is global and unconditional; it resonates in the *nommo* and the rhythm of lyrics that make you want to dance:

> I shall arise in the morning
> I shall witness the dawning of a new day for Africa
> I shall arise in the morning to the sound of the drums
> I shall come Mother Africa
> I shall come
> I shall come

Her tepid language and use of Jamaican dialect and modes of expression gives a musicality to her poems as subtle as a tropical breeze, though there is little subtlety in the message of the music that comes across with the clarity of thunder. Love, peace, African unity, heritage, revolution, this is the way the world turns on an axis of imagination and energy put forth from a visionary's pen. Farika Berhane is that visionary poet whose artworks have been reified in publications in Jamaica, London, the United States, and the presentation of numerous awards including four Jamaican Literary Festival awards, the International Black Writers Contest (London), several DC Commission of the Arts awards, and a Lifetime Achievement Literary award for the 50th anniversary of Jamaican Independence. In the ancient world, in every culture, poetry and music were inseparable. Nana Farika restores the unity of poetry and music with a prosody that promises only the unpredictable, soft and salient, traditional yet modern and always in the moment. The past is presented as a springboard to a future of irrefutable victory.

Dr. Nubia Kai
Assistant Professor,
Department of Drama, Howard University

Author's Foreword

This collection of poetry demanded to be written. I did not plan writing it. It emerged and took on a life of its own. It marks the first time that I have reached out to the Caribbean/Jamaican communities in the island and its Diaspora in a publication since my migration to the United States. I have set out to share different aspects of my cultural insights, memories, stories of growing up in the island of Jamaica and its Diaspora in New York. It is a step towards utilizing the worldwide interest in Jamaican culture and patois to pick up the threads of works that have been on the backburner.

Like many Jamaicans, I was schooled in appreciating patois through attending concerts by Jamaican folklore icon, Louise Bennett and listening to her radio programs. She was a family friend and so I had the good fortune of knowing her personally and receiving guidance and praise from her for my writing. Her husband Eric Coverley had the same birthday as my father and they often shared birthday gatherings. They were both born on July 23rd, the birth date of His Imperial Majesty, Emperor Haile Selassie I of Ethiopia.

Louise Bennett used to make appearances at our

neighborhood community concerts. I remember that the women who arranged the concerts always referred to her as Louise but when the governor's wife came to our benefits it was always Lady this and Lady that. After a long absence created by my journey into Rastafari, I finally reunited with Louise Bennett by phone and requested her to do the preface for my poetry book on Black Freedom. She readily consented but died before I could send her the manuscript. The dialect poems and the inside out journey into the cultural mindset of the Jamaican people is testimony of the influence of Miss Lou on me.

The works in *I-Lan' in di Sun* date from the late 1960's to April 2014. They map my journey into consciousness, awakened by two sojourns into the Caribbean communities in New York, one as a teenager just out of high school in the late 1950's and the other in the 1960's. I not only lived in the West Indian community but in the East village among artists, seeing the Black Arts Movement and the peace movement. Studying at the Instituto de Allende in Guanajuato, Mexico in the 1960's and traveling to Dar es Salaam, Tanzania during the 1970's were high spots along my journey. In Mexico my horizons broadened by interacting with ancient Native American cultures.

I reside in Washington DC due to prevailing conditions in Jamaica that made me leave the island in the late 1970's, and restricted my freedom to practice my craft as a journalist. Before taking up residence in Washington DC, I lived in California for a decade. During that time I worked as a performing artist with the Nairobi Institute of Cultural Arts, and with the California Poets in Schools as an arts educator. I also worked as a cultural ethnographic researcher for Stanford University, the Institute for the Study of Black Family Life and Culture, and UC Berkeley.

When I migrated to America I found little interest in Jamaican patois and was unable to get a cast together for my award winning play. My plays and radio/television/film scripts were written in the Jamaican patois, the language of my heart. Most of my poetry since the 1970's were written in standard English and geared towards awakening the consciousness of African peoples. The journey of writing *I-Lan' in di Sun* called for me to return to the time and space of Jamaica and its Diaspora.

I open the collection with the poem *We Are Our Ancestors*, which speaks of the Maroons of Jamaica perception of themselves. The Maroon anthem is very popular among African American audiences. *An Anthem for the Jamaican People* is an affirmation of the best characteristics the Jamaican people see themselves possessing and is very popular with them. All audiences love the magic and mystery of Grandi Nanni (Nanny). She unites all in her spell.

Each section of the book addresses a particular theme of my journey and the life of the Jamaican people. *A Jamaican Childhood* celebrates the island's beauty, its folklore, seasons and people through a child's eyes. The section entitled *Family Ties* introduces the reader to my family background. This section was written specifically for audiences curious about what helped to mold me into who I am. It documents the lives and times of rapidly changing Jamaica and helps to pass on the realty of a time that is no more. I have especially included poem snapshots of World War II with this in mind.

My family, like many in Jamaica has ties outside the island. They migrated to Cuba, Panama, United States Canada, and England. The poems, *The Man from Panama* and *Viva Cuba* give glimpses into Latino connections in my family. In the section *In Search of Betta Mus' Come in Foreign Lands*, my poems reveal the lives and aspirations of English speaking Caribbean people in the United States, focused on the Jamaicans. The poems *It was on those nights* and *Dem Old-time West Indians* celebrate aspects of the life of the Caribbean community during the 1950's and 1960's. *We are the Jewmaycans* addresses the islanders acquisitiveness, boldness and daring, qualities that propels them on the world scene in spite of the size of their country.

Selected poems in *A Love that Died* are reflective and quietly insightful. Rastafari traditionally did not celebrate death and so many have not had the opportunity to mourn their loss when loved ones pass. These poems allow me to say good-bye. They are inspired by my journey and work within the Maroon communities of Jamaica. In these communities the dead are not dead but alive in spirit forever to guide the living. The poem *Let me Lay you to Rest* is based on a Maroon Akan ritual song sung at the burying of a loved one.

In the section about *Social Conditions* in Jamaica my poems reveal the grinding poverty and murder that Black youths in the island's ghettos face. *The Smell of Death* gives a graphic picture of Kingston as an armed camp sucking the life of urban youths while their mothers wonder about the futility of raising them for death.

Message from the Ghettos is a cry from youths for help from those who claim to be working on their behalf. It was inspired by my play *On the Third Day H.I.M Rise*.

In the section *Hail Jah Rastafari*, the poem *I-Lan' in di Sun* addresses Rastafari focus on repatriation, race redemption and the sometimes love/hate relationship with the island of their birth. Glimpses of the female journey and vision of Rastafari and her spiritual role are shown in such poems as *Call I Sistah Love*, *Di Road to Mt. Zion*, *The Rastafari Queen*, and *Woman Clothed with the Sun*. The poem *Christ, the Rastaman* shows the spiritual role of the Rastafari male before the advent of Bob Marley and the singing stars who now headline the Rastafari movement. The hard road to travel as a Rastafari through the persecution endured in the island of Jamaica comes to life in *A Living Sacrifice of Love*, and *Rainbows of The Promised Land*.

The concluding section *Writing my Soul* gives the reader glimpses into my soul as a writer pouring sun-drenched rain words from my inner being.

Nana Farika Berhane

ANTHEMS AND ANCESTRAL VOICES

Nanny of the Maroons

We Are Our Ancestors

(An Anthem for the Maroon People)

We are our Ancestors

They live through our being

Though unseen

They are not dead

Not history's forgotten

Brought to life only through those

Seeking fame from our name

Our forefathers

Our foremothers

LIVE!

They are not dead

Not skeletons on moldy shelves

In books seldom read

Our abeng still blows freedom calls

Summoning the ancestors here

Awakening the past

Conquering ancestral death

Breathing life in our ancestors

Our drums echo ancestral heartbeats

Ritually

Speaking to us, through us

With us

Vibrating freedom sounds

Arousing the ancestors

Our dreams conjure them nocturnally

Guiding/confiding/whispering

Plotting/plodding

Revealing clues to us

About us

Clues about them

Ensuring freedom's continuity

Through their blood legacy in our genes

We are our Ancestors.

Year 1995, Washington DC

An Anthem for the Jamaican People

We are a loving people
Faces uplifted towards the sun
Making our mark on Black History

Quite out of proportion
To the size of the island we come from
We love the rock that we were born on
But will travel the world
To fulfill our ambition

We are a hardworking people
Faces upturned towards the sun
Leaving our imprint on time's sand

We incubate sprinters
Who become world champions
We produce great thinkers, writers
Artists and world class musicians

We are a determined people
Who are often the stone
Babylon buck it toe on
We keep the faith that

Better will come

That we will overcome

And our trials and tribulations

Will soon be gone

Year 2013, Paul Laurence Dunbar Apts., Washington DC

Grandi Nanni Lives

Ancestral

Blood ties

Sing of her

Pouring libations

To the invisible/visible

Town leader

Who watches over them

In mountain villages

Over the centuries

The eternal mother

(ii)

Her spirit hovers in Moore Town

In songs, dances, dreams

And rituals

Secret practices

They hold

In New Nanny Town

I am told

A bird bears her name
A type of house
Carries her fame

The Nanny River
Ever knowing, ever flowing
Pregnant with secrets

That can summon her here
To appear
From Stony River
"Grandi Nanni Come ya
Come from Stony Rivah
Yu bring bwoy, yu bring gyal ... "
And then disappear
The elusive river mother

(iii)
In the hush of tropical nights
When crickets chirp
Keeping time's rhythm
With internal clocks

Tales of magic are told

And mysteries unfold

About a woman

Who was a military strategist

And outwitted Brutish Brutan

In the seventeen hundreds

Yet had/has such a soft touch

And knows how to endure

In tip toe

In the hearts of her *Yoyo*

(iv)

Through her

Time's barriers crumble

Long ago and far away tumble

Into present day reality

She makes

Ancient Maroon spirits rise

Disguised

In ambush mode

Clothed as trees

They spring

On unsuspecting
Redcoats and Black shot traitors

Blow the abeng!
Her Nyankipong warriors
Are victorious again!

December 2013, Long Island, Jamaica, New York
(quoted excerpt from Grandi Nanni folk song in italics)

(v)
Queen magically calling me
Elusive one of mystery
Dwelling in the Blue Mountains cunningly
Trap cultural invaders in your magic pot
Don't allow them to find
The stronghold of our mind
Succor us so our weary souls find rest
For in you we are blessed
True wonder woman of the west

The 1990's, Washington DC

FAMILY TIES

My Family in the 1950's

Aunt Regina

Aunt Regina did once 'ave a husban'
But afta him lef' ahr fi a faas' Kingston gyal
Wid a big backside
An' breasts stickin' out mos' indecent

Shi sell ahr married ring
An' pour ahr soul out in cultivatin' ahr lan'
An' raisin' a army a bwoy an' gyal pickney
Dough shi 'ave no pickney a ahr own

Shi put a stap to people a-call ahr mule
An' show dem she get di blessin'
As di village matriarch

Year 1989, Washington DC

Sundays with Father

On Sundays he would get up
At the crack of dawn
Get the newspaper from the walkway
Go into the bathroom with it
Then he'd take a bath and dress himself for church
instead of work.

My mother never went to church with him
But we always did
(We had no choice)
Father went everywhere late but tried to be on time
For church
"You'll be late for heaven," mother always remarked
"When you go to heaven
St. Peter will shut the gate
In you face because you late."

Father wanted to walk into church
Surrounded by us five children
A father to be admired by the full congregation
He'd shout at us, scold us, bully us
Get into the car and begin blowing the car horn
Continuously

Waking up the sleeping people in the neighborhood

From their Sunday morning rest

Because He, was going to church

On time

The racket never ceased to embarrass mother

Who would scurry us out of the house

And shove us into the car to end the confusion

When church was over

After he met with his church friends

And the priests and the business acquaintances

He wanted to impress

After he had put us on show

He set out to return home

Driving as usual in the middle of the road

Among his other road infractions

Annoying the hell out of other motorists.

Upon arriving safely home in spite of his bad driving

He was served breakfast by the helper

Or my mother on her days off

He always ate heartily

He'd go out on business visits

That required my brother to drive him
Or he'd recline in his lounge chair
Smoking a cigarette or dozing
While mother lectured him about how
he was killing his lungs
And he ignored her

Year 2009, South Dakota Ave, Washington DC.

Viva Cuba (i)

We were dancing at a Jamaican/Cuban party

When we heard the news

The music stopped

Hooray throats shouted

Our hopes for the revolution

The dawn of justice in creation

Up with Fidel Castro

The victory was won

We danced our joy

In New York at that party

I was there with my Cuban born cousins

Today I don't know if they are living or dead

But on that night when we cheered

The revolution

We were so close in meditation

Year 2013, Paul Laurence Dunbar Apts., Washington DC

Viva Cuba (ii)

It was a time when Cuba was just a stone throw
from Jamaica
We used to take boats and go there frequently
There was a constant trekking to and fro you know

It was like going from one side of the island to the other
Closer in distance
For Christ's sake
Only ninety miles away

On a clear day
You could see Cuba's Jeweled coast
from certain parts of Jamaica

Americans were running things then
There was work and good pay
Especially if you could speak and understand English
Before the Great Depression

My Aunt Asaneth lived there with her handsome St. Lucian
Husband and their two boys
Before leaving for America
The land of the free

Where she discovered blacks
Could not be all they wanted to be

She bonded with Cuban/Caribbean ones
Cheering Batista's downfall
Until Castro fell out with America
And they abandoned ship

Jamaica was no longer a near dear little sister to Cuba
Cuba's jeweled coast no longer sparkled in her sun
It was obscured by black clouds
Its ninety miles proximity
Became a secret world
And many Jamaicans living there
Headed home

But my father that rebel in Jamaica refused to bow.
He said Castro was right
To put up a fight for sovereignty
And named his fiercest black dog
Castro.

Year 2013, Paul Laurence Dunbar Apts., Washington DC

The Man from Panama

The man from Panama was so dashing
He was so suave
How he could flatter
And make the ladies heart flutter

The man from Panama
Got hold of my grandmother's photo
Posted on some social page
He fell in love with it
And swore he must have her

No longer protected by her father's
Tongue lashing against idle chatter
She answered his letters
Beautifully written
And became smitten

Letters flowed from Panama
Praising her beauty and intellect
He proposed to come to Jamaica
To marry her and carry her
Into a life of ecstasy

She dressed exquisitely
To meet him when his ship came in
He walked on the deck so dapper
So handsome, enquiring of grandma
"Are you pleased with the gentleman?"

It was never told me what she replied
But she married the man from Panama
Who took her from her home in Port Antonio
To live in Kingston city
Where they had two boy babies
Who died in their cribs, such a pity
I do not know their gravesites

The man from Panama had a roving eye
He tried to tame her
And she tried to shame him
To seek work aggressively
Instead of laying in bed
Playing in her thick wooly hair
Talking sweet talk or flirting with passing women

The marriage did not go well
The sudden deaths of the babies began to tell
As did his emphasis of stepping out on the town
Grandma would get dressed and step out too
Even if she had nowhere to go, she'd put on a show
He did not like that
They had many a spat

The man from Panama disappeared one day
He did not stay
He up and went away
Back to Panama they say.

Year 2013, Paul Laurence Dunbar Apts., Washington DC

A Child Is Born

On my way from the St. Andrew hills to the Trench Town
Maternity home for child birth
We ran into a road block
"Three o'clock, road block
Hey Mr. Cop, ain't got no birth certificate on me now"

Police with menacing guns
Shone blinding light in our eyes
Barked demanding orders for
The car certificate and license
"Could not recognize the faces standing over me
They were all dressed in uniforms of brutality"

They searched our car and those of
Other resigned motorists
Who like us, were caught in their trap
"Ambush in di night
Protected by His Majesty."

Labour Pains racked me
Seeing my condition – learning of my destination
Not wanting to deal with the imminent birth of my child
We were released

to continue on our journey to Trench Town
"Trench Town rock, don't watch that"
"Trench Town rock, you reap what you sow"

So there we were in Trench Town
Bob Marley and the Wailers wailing
Through pregnant women everywhere
Weeping and moaning they seemed to appear
"Weeping an' a wailing tonight
Oh, can't stop the tears"
Out of the dimness, out of nowhere
Sobbing and crying their pain in the night
Some women in despair and some in fright

I settled down among the crowd in the night
Awaiting my call
Pacing the hall
Taking it in all
The policeman's wife crying
for her dead husband who had been shot
The dry labour pain searing
mixed with the concrete of her grief
"Trench Town rock, I'd never let the children cry
Cause you got to tell Jah-Jah why"

The amply built matron
Returnee from England
Doing a thriving business in delivering babies
Shooing away fathers disturbing her woman birth rituals

My turn came for the mini bus line up of women
On the birth table with several babies' auras
Lingering
There I am
Cries of recent birth arrivals
Wailing through the Trench Town night
"Weeping an' a wailing tonight"

I had to work, work, work, to get out my baby
He was so cool with the warmth of my insides
Not interested to leave the cozy for the unknown
Push! Push! Push! Push out his big head
No relaxation, the nurse screaming
"You'll strangle your baby," as I relaxed
Thinking that once the head was out
The rest of him would follow as is usual
But he was stuck!

I had to push out his broad shoulders

His side, his chubby legs

All nine pounds of him

What exhaustion!

"Labour is work.

Why do you think its called labour?"

The nurse shared her creed

Finally it was over.

He was out!

The cucumber cool baby!

Overcome by exhaustion,

Sleep overtook me

The nurse again scolding

This time for feeding and ensuring bonding

And announcing of the banished father

Who looked at Mr. Cool and said

"Congratulations."

Year 2012, Paul Laurence Dunbar Apts., Washington DC

*(italic quotes from songs "Three O'Clock Roadblock",
"Ambush in the Night," "Burnin' and Lootin'," and
"Trench Town Rock"* by Bob Marley and the Wailers)

Aunt Rachel

Aunt Rachel saved my life my mother said

When she was sick on the hospital bed

Lingering in the twilight of sanity

Suffering from the effects of a nervous breakdown

Labeled as crazy by bad minded women

Jealous of the attention

The handsome brown doctor was giving her

My grandmother could not cope

She did not know how to stop my constant crying

How to get me to eat

Or nourish my wounded spirit

I was dwindling away fast

They didn't expect me to last

I was pure skin and bones

Down from a hefty nine pounder at birth

Every day she expected to hear news

That I was dead

It never happened, instead

I kept on living, though on a thread

Until rescued by Aunt Rachel

Who blessed my child presence
In her childless home

Aunt Rachel was my grandmother's half sister
Great grandfather had her
With an East Indian woman
He had a touch of Indian blood too
And Aunt Rachel grew up to marry
A full Indian named Babu

I dimly remember her coming to our home
She always carried a basket with fruits I adored
She was slim and cheerful
And hardly visited after awhile

Mother was always dropping hints about her
Influence on me
How I liked to sit cross-legged like her
And liked bright colors
Instead of ladylike pastels
And that she saved my life.

In my teens I began feeling that I needed to see her
I nagged and nagged until father gave in
To my pleas to take me to the woman
Who saved my life

She lay sick and emaciated
But was joyful to see us
Such warmth through her illness
It lighted the room with its blaze
She was amazed
To see how tall and strong I had grown

I was not going to see her alive again
I knew it
There was a dark shadow
Beneath the brightness of her smile

Dad and I lingered awhile
Then left, sadness weighing on my heart
Blinding tears made me stumble
Walking in the brilliance of the sun
Aimlessly beside father
Along the rusting zinc fenced dirt lane

"What *yu crying for? Father asked.*
She soon get better. Yu too sentimental."
But she did not get better
She died not long after we saw her
And her husband Babu died the following week
They were inseparable, even in death

We did not attend their funerals
They were poor people
It wasn't required of us
And grandma didn't insist
To see off her Indian sis.

Year 2012

The Mystery of Mother (i)

She remained always
A mystery

Large dreamy eyes
Looking absently
Beautiful
In their distance

Year 2013, Paul Laurence Dunbar Apts., Washington DC

Land and Flowers

He would drive around gazing

Lovingly at empty lots of land

Dreaming of ownership

He could see houses rising from them

Blood line success

Empires of progress

But mother saw sun gardens

Trees and flowers growing

Year 2014, Paul Laurence Dunbar Apts., Washington DC

The Garden of My Mother

The garden of her longed for flowers
A tropical fullness of them
She planted red roses of many shades
Pink ones also
Orchids, marigolds, gardenias, Joseph Coats in her garden
Pomegranate, grapefruit and orange trees
at the side of her front yard

Also East Indian and Bombay table mangoes
But Black mangoes and hairy mangoes
Being common, were planted at the back
And left unprotected from children's constant attack

I was a fruitarian living off the common mangoes
Sweet, sweet black mangoes
Lovely hairy mangoes whose hair stick in your teeth

I dwelt among a wonderland of flowers, fruits and greenery
This was the scenery of my yard
My mother's legacy

April 2014, Paul Laurence Dunbar Apts., Washington DC

The Mystery of Mother (ii)

Quiet like pools of water were her eyes

Deep with mysteries

Far from our everyday problems and cares

She lived a child bride

Giving birth out of season

(iii)

We children like baby birds

Mouths outstretched open

Bid her come home from distant past lands

with mother nourishments

March 2014, Paul Laurence Dunbar Apts., Washington DC

She was a Flower

She was a flower blowing in the wind
Blooming plants at her touch
She loved them so much

She was happiest in her love garden
Birthing flowers that leapt and swirled
Magnificently in her sun

She was a flower blowing in the wind of time
She was mother.

March 2014, Paul Laurence Dunbar Apts., Washington DC

Gan-Gan, My Father's Mother

Gan-Gan was my father's mother
Thin with small black eyes
That did not miss a thing
A farmer from hillside country of rural St. Andrew
Who loved her land

Her mother was enslaved as a child
And her grandmother suffered slavery's cruel wiles
Gan-Gan carried within her
Ancestral songs, dances, intertwined with Christianity
From the motherland
While married in the church to Grandpa George Hamilton

She was the champion flogger in her community
She ran her household under law and authority
Children knew her rules, she taught them well
And wrote down each infraction in a book

You knew her cup was overflowing
And you were in for some flogging
When you heard Gan-Gan humming
You trembled like leaf expecting the whirlwind
The tamarind switch that stung so much

Gan-Gan raised her children to be God fearing

Her name was Sarah and her donkey was Sari

Sari was her limousine

She and Sari were a team

Ill-treat Sari and you knew how she could be mean

She banished her own son Michael

For riding Sari on a spree to Kingston

You wouldn't believe the scandal on the land

That came from Sarah Hamilton

I remember her as a gentle soul

Who loved me to comb and plait her hair

She said my touch relaxed her

And she would nod and doze

Cousin Enid liked to send me packing

Grumbling about pickney playing in Gan-Gan hair

And that Gan-Gan turn into a toothless lioness

What a shame

She become so tame

But who knows, maybe Gan-Gan always had that side

That she hide from prying eyes

To make sure her children survived.

Year 2012, Paul Laurence Dunbar Apts., Washington DC

My Aunt Mabel

Like a cackling hen
Gurgling rivers gushing from hillsides
Rejoicing peasants
Loud, raucous, joy reveling
Revealing memories of ancestral lands
Vast jungles, lands expressive of lungs expansive
Where one could let laughter ring out
For miles and miles and receive answers
From trees and animals in the wild
Thus was Mabel's laughter
Matched only by her brother's - my father

Harlem Streets could not dampen it
No matter how much grime it heaped on it
It survived wintry blasts
And betrayed her disguise, posing as a Black American
Come to visit Jamaica
Recommended by her friend Mabel
The laughter rang out and everyone knew
She couldn't hide
"Yu mean you don't know me Aubrey?" Mabel inquired
Then she laughed and hear mi father now
"Is you that Mabel? Mabel is you that?"

(ii)

As wintry winds blew in Harlem

Aunt Mabel would make herbal brews

In huge pots, tasting and stirring

To keep sickness at bay

I came to know Harlem through her

Lodge brothers, teachers, preachers

And drug dealers, number runners too

She was Miss Mabel to them

(iii)

Decades before she died

Aunt Mabel had her gravesite prepared

And put headstone on it that read

"Mabel Rose May you rest in Peace,"

While she walkin' pon earth quite contented

People said that the duppy dem think

She dead aready so dem noh come fi ahr

She trick dem

She live till she was ova ninety

Walkin' about quite sprightly

And never dead till she was force to leave Harlem.

Year 2012, St. Andrew, Jamaica

A JAMAICAN CHILDHOOD

My Brothers, Sister and I

Silva yu I-Lan' Worl' (i)

Heaven open up
So pour dung waata outa sky
Rain breeze a-blow
Silva green waata soak trees

Wite lightning a-flash
Yunda a-growl an' a-roll
Making earsplitting clap

Muddy waata a-flow 'pon di street dem
Mek bicycle dem bee-bop
An' drop, bip bop
An' bicycle ridah dem
Splish splash

Cahr engine splutta
An' cawf, an' stop
An' young man dem
Get hustling fi push dem
An' say, "Tank God,"
Fi di rain blessin'

Year 1978, East Palo Alto, California

Silva yu I-Lan' Worl' (ii)

Gyal pickney yu run

Run eena di school yard

Run eena di street

Octoba rain pon yu face

Warm an' 'evy

Gyal pickney, off wid yu shoes

Off wid yu socks

Jine dem bwoy dem

Sail stick boat dem

Pon dem street dem

Now a riva

Gyal pickney

Yu boat come out fus'

Yu win! Yu win!

Who las' is a big jackass

Octoba rain runnin' ova yu face

An' di wool, das yu face

It wet-up yu eye-lash dem

So silva yu i-lan' worl.

Year 1978, East Palo Alto, California

Butterfly Memories

Butterflies flapping wings in the sun
Fluttering in fields of buttercups
Yellow butterflies, yellow sun
Sea of yellow meets my child's eyes
Yellow, yellow everywhere

Sunlight flickering through trees
As I chase them, then, surprise!
Right before my very eyes
They are joined by rainbow ones
Multitudes swarming everywhere
Flitter, flutter without care

On dusty and paved roads
Fluttering rainbow butterflies
I catch one, hold it in my hands
Have so much childish fun
Running with it in the sun
Childhood laughter explodes

I release it, watch it soar
Oh how I wish like carefree butterflies
I could fly - free.

August 2013, Newcastle, Jamaica

Peeni Walli Poem

Peeni Walli, candle flies
Peeni Walli, fireflies
Lightning bugs
Lanterns for the darkest nights
Helping to drive away fright

Catch them and put them in bottles
Don't forget to punch holes in the caps
So Peeni Walli can breathe
Dem mek such lovely toys
Fi country gyal an' boys

But plenty big people tink dem is duppy
An' trow dem wey a bush
No matter how di pickney dem bawl

Ongly a-tell dem bwoy an'gyal
Fi shut dem mowt
Or dem wi give dem sinting
To shout about

Peeni Walli, fireflies
Green light, yellow light fire sparks
Shining on rolling calf
Three foot horse
An' all dem tings

Mek dem duppy dem tek flight
An' everyting turn out alright
For dose who don't have electric light

August 2013, Newcastle, Jamaica

Augus' Mawnin' Come Agen

Augus' mawnin' come agen

Jubilation in di air

Ankcestor dem rise an' draw near

Dem nah 'ave noh fear

To visit wi an' appear

As janga eena riva

An' fish eena sea

An' eena rockstone

An' eena bush, an' tree

An' eena man 'art

So walk 'bout like smady

As dem do annually

Come young, come old

Come boy, come gyal

Come all smady

Come an' tek part in di commemoration

Of Black people liberation

Tru dem emancipation

From di evil of slavery

(ii)

Augus' mawning dawn once more

Once agen wi mus member di fus proclamation

"Jubilee! Jubilee! Queen Victoria

Set wi free!"

Pickney come larn yu history

Bout wat yu Ankcestors

Had was to do fi guarantee

Dem was set free

Mek wi glad bag bus'

At wi Victoria victory.

Year 2013, Paul Laurence Dunbar Apts., Washington DC

Ring Game Memories

Gyal pickney singing an' chanting ring games

emotions a-run high

bye bye

"Mi luv will yu 'ave mi to pick a rose"

spirit rise

"into dis beautiful garden"

chilehood jus' a fleetin' dream

Yu wake up one mawning an' it gone'

too soon

What a shame

Who is to blame?

Why wi caahn stay in dat time

forevah?

(quotes from ring game "Jane and Louisa will soon come home")

(ii)

"There's a brown girl in di ring

tra la la la laa

sweet like sugar

an' nice like spice"

Ring games wi sing 'bout browning

So wat bout di black gyal?

Wha' 'appen to di Black gyal song?

Shi noh sweet to?

Wha' 'appen to di Black Gyal ting

Why all di sing 'bout browning?

Why Black always undah attack

an get tell fi stay back?

March 2014, Paul Laurence Dunbar Apts., Washington DC

(quote from ring game "There's a Brown Girl in di Ring")

War Time Jamaica

War plane a-fly ova Jamaica

Zeppelin plane dem up high eena wi sky

War deh inna Englan' an' wi is it colony

Food deh pon ration

Beef an' rice an' all tings nice

Pickney mek saying dat go

"Yu tink yu nice, Yu tink yu nice

Yu tink yu nice

Like a poun' a rice?"

Grandma complaining

An' buyin' tings from di Black Market

Hooligan an' riff raff a-run it shi say

But shi kip going back

for shi 'ave high ches' fi beef an' rice

(ii)

Wite people a-fight Worl' War in farrin lans'

An' a-axe wi come join eena it

Or Garman man may come a-Jamaica come kill wi

Wat a sinting!

Miss Nellie di walk bout brown lady news carrier

a-cry pon moonlight night for it mek wi in plain sight

Garman plane cyahn si wi

No matta ow di man wey a-walk street bawl out

"Tun off yu light! Tun off yu light"

Garman man cyahn si wi in di moonlight night

Blackout a-come often

Sudden-sudden widout warnin'

It can tek yu in the moving theater an' you haffi go home

For pitcher gone

Blackout! Blackout pon di lan

Wi haffi 'ide from Garman

Wi pickney play war game in wi yard

But sad it is to see pitcher of Jamaica soljah

Who dead overseas fighting to kip wi free

(iii)

War done! War done!

Soljah a-come 'ome

Soljah a-come in plenty soljah lorry

Hundred upon hundred a-dem a come 'ome

Some a dem drunk

Some a dem bruk

Noh even 'ave money fi pay fare pon tram car

Wat is dis?

A so dem treat wi afta wi put wi life pon di line fi dem?

A so dem do wi?

March 2014, Paul Laurence Dunbar Apts., Washington DC

Summers with Aunt Geraldine

Me a magaw chile
Runnin' wile
Up an' down green mountainside
Jumpin' riva banks
Skippin' on the brown path dem'

Listenin' to Hope Riva gurgle
Summa nights with Peeni Walli light
Stars hangin' so near in di sky
Yu feel yu can touch dem if yu try
Walkin' in bright moonlight
Silva, Silva everywhere

Me, a city chile
Walkin' pon mountainside
Spendin' time in country
Learnin' how to balance pails of waata
Pon wi head, run wid it like country cousin

Without spillin' a drop
Waata in di pail help
Full di waata barrel fi drink
Si mi now a-walk up steep hill

Steppin' 'pon log step
Fun an' duty intertwine

If wi spill di waata
Wi haffi mek more trips to di riva
Wi glad so till
Wen rain come poundin' dung
An' spare wi from carry waata
From di riva

Eatin' juicy mangoes
From crocus bags in Auntie hilltop yard
Sittin' on a tree stump
Revelin' mango sweetness
Bright orange
Drippin' pon mi cloze
Hearin' Aunt Geraldine a-shout
"Ben' ova gyal! Ben ova!
Doah mek mango juice stain yu cloze!"

Den listenin' for the treat in store
Aunt Geraldine amazin' change
From strict disciplinarian to storytellah
Capturin' Brer Anansi, Brer Tigah
Asuno, an' Tukuma in pantomime
Brer dawg an' puss to
Sistah Fowl an' cockroach
Mekin' dem walk before mi eyes
How Aunt Geraldine bring dem characters alive

Plungin' us headlong into African folklore
That cross Atlantic Ocean to Caribbean shores
On ships wid wi ancestors in chains of slavery
As we children beg
For more story!
More! More! More!

Year 2012, Bath, St. Thomas, Jamaica

Riva Bath

Dashin' dung windin' hillside path
Sweet breeze blowin'
Sunlight glowin'
As you 'ed fi di riva·
So tek off you cloze

Splish! Splash
Yu jump in
Sunlight streamin'
Beamin' pon yu
A i-lan' pickney

Summa breeze flowin'
Yu dive undah di waata
So cool an' so fresh
Yu hide undah it from sunhot

Cool man
Mi gaan.

Year 2010, Paul Laurence Dunbar Apts., Washington DC

Green Hills of Jamaica

Green Hills of Jamaica
That sheltered me in the cocoon of my childhood
Green hills of Jamaica who gave me rain
Green Hills of Jamaica that comfort my pain
Green hills of Jamaica who preserve Africa for me

Green hills of Jamaica
Green hills, green hills
Green Hills of Jamaica

Year 1971, Green Hills, Portland, Jamaica

Jamaica Lullaby

Sleep Jamaica, sleep
Sleep, mi i-lant sleep

Di sweetes' fruit is di wan
Dat stan longes' in di sun
Dem dey fruit
Dat ripe too soon
Force-ripe
An' get blight

So mi country
Mi pretty i-lant country
Mi pretty-pretty black gyal
Tek yu time ripe in di sun

Tek yu time ripe
No bada run
Sleep in chilewood
As lang as yu cyahn
Sleep mi i-lant, sleep
Sleep Jamaica, sleep

Year 1971, East Palo Alto, California

Childhood Nanni Ring Game

"String needle, string needle

Long, long thread

Nanni show mi how yu string di needle

Long, long thread

Thread oh, thread oh

Long, long thread

Nanni show mi how yu string di needle

Long, long thread."

Example of Grandi Nanni in children's ring games showing herself not only as the revolutionary, mystic, magical and military strategist, but as a Mother leader/teacher of children's games through the ages.

Mother Nanni Show Wi

Di play begin
An' di ball gone 'roun
Mother Nanni show wi 'ow di ball gone 'roun

Yu pass di ball
An' di ball gone 'roun
Mother Nanni show wi how di ball gone 'roun

Play ball, play ball
Play ball, play
Mother Nanni show wi 'ow di ball gone roun'

Example of Grandi Nanni in children's ring games showing herself not only as the revolutionary, mystic, magical and military strategist but as a Mother leader/teacher of children's games through the ages.

Carefree Childhood

Long leg chocolate child

Chasing the wind in your hillside

Sweating shiny rainbows in the heat of the sun

Having so much fun

You and nature being one

Experiencing exhilarating joy

Year 1995, Washington DC

SOCIAL CONDITIONS

Rural Clarendon, Jamaica

Let di Soun' Systems Play

Do, offisah, do
Noh mash an' crash wi voice
Noh out wi night time self
Dat sing wi pain a belly
Wi pain a 'art
In music so sweet
Wi haffi move wi dancin' feet
Night afta night afta night
Till it mad di earshole a Babylon

From the play *On the Third Day H.I.M Rise,*
Year 1970, Green Hills, Portland, Jamaica.

Rum Drinkers Blues

Wen evening fall
Wen evening fall
Wi drownded out wi tiday
Wi drownded out yesiday
Wi drownded out wi tomarra
Wi drownded out wi sarra
Wi drownded wi bruk pocket state

(Rent due, school fee due
Pickney need food
Wey wi gwine do?)

Wi wash out wi mind
An' flush all tings clean
Wid di rum
Di evil wite rum

From the play *On the Third Day H.I.M. Rise,*
Year 1970, Green Hills, Portland, Jamaica

The Smell Of Death

When I was young the smell of death was far
I had to make a special excursion
in order to meet him

Today, death sits at our tables
Death rides our highways
Gunmen are on the prowl
Oh listen to the howls of bereaved mothers

Funeral rites
Are familiar sights
Death hangs like a pall
Over our land for all to see

Armed soldiers/police
Parade our streets
In order to keep death's class low
So he will not make a show
of climbing up
to barricaded St. Andrew

Boys practice
Firing pistols, M16's
Like toys

Using ratchet knives

To bring

Death

To others

Who are their

Brothers

Funeral rites

Are familiar sights

The stench of death

Burns the nostrils in the ghettos

Death

Is the companion of everyone there

Everyday

They fear

As he goes on the loose

But black mothers ponder

And they wonder

At the wisdom of raising Black youths

To watch them meet

Death

In the streets

July 1973, Jack's Hill, St. Andrew, Jamaica

Message from the Ghettos

Inspecta! Inpecta!

Dem a-kill mi inspecta!

Time to stap talkin'

Time to shut yu book

Open yu yeye

Stap inspectin'

Start doin'

Something

To save mi

From deadin'!!

INSPECTA!!!

From the play *On the Third Day H.I.M. Rise,*
Year 1970, Green Hills, Portland, Jamaica

Dreamin' di Impossible

Dreamin'

Di impossible in summerlan'

Wi blas'

Bing Crosby white Christmas song

Wen Christmastime cum

An' put up

Snow trimmin'

In di blazin' sun

The 1990's, Washington DC

.

Who Trubble Nawma?

A who trubble Nawma?

Yu si ahr of late?

Gyal, a caahn relate

How di good 'oman pickney a-carry ahrself

Shi tek up black people bizness 'pon ahr 'ed

Mek ahr good-good 'air dred

Tun Rasta gyal.

Well sah

Di good-lookin' gyal

It mek mi so sad

Dat di gyal tun out so unconshionable

Afta ahr parents strain

Fi gi ahr good heducation

A who trubble Nawma?

Yu si 'ow shi vex up ahr face

Wid respectable people mi dear

Like shi a-declare war 'pon dem?

Ongly walkin' 'rung tung wid ole wutless Nayga

An' mi 'ear seh nobady wi gi ahr a wuk

Wid all ahr good heducation

Mi noh blame dem yu 'ear
All like mi woulda fear
Fi 'ave smady look like dat
Eena mi nice nice office

Wat ah mean seh yu know wat Rasta gi
Smoke an' chat all day long
'Bout Afrika an' Etiopialan'
Like seh wi is any African
Jamaica tuff but it sweet
Who waan' lef' it fi meet
Wile lion an' tigah eena African jungle?

Aah mi dear
It grieve mi fi true
To see ahr 'eding to walk an' talk to ahrself
An' ded eena mad howse or poor owse or jail
Or mek smady kill ahr

Look pon great great Marcus Garvey
Shi tink shi cyahn succeed wen man like dat fail?
Dem sell 'im out fi rice an' peas, if yu please
Wen yu tek up Black people bizness pon yu 'ed
Yu will ded in despair
Unless yu noh fear
Fi chat wan ting an' do di apposite

Lissen mam, please talk to ahr yu 'ear
So shi wi stop do as shi declare
But is who trubble Nawma dough eh?

Year 1975, Duhaney Park, Kingston, Jamaica

The Party is Over

A woman weeps
Her cries take wings
On Trade Winds
Blowing from the Caribbean Sea

A child puzzles
At the sight and smell of her
Charred flesh
And burn bubbles jiggling

The woman was brought to her home
On a stretcher
People said her party headquarters
Where she worked was burnt down
While she was in it
Shorty before the island's
First general election
Under Adult Suffrage

Symbolic of things to come?
She will no longer teach the child
and her siblings
How to spin gigs

Play games

sing party songs

Her party is over.

Year 2013, Paul Laurence Dunbar Apts., Washington DC

The Time is Now

Time to feed the hungry
NOW!
Time to clothe the naked
NOW!
Time for man to tek yah
Tun Jamaica into
JAHMEKYA!

Hurl di rainbow in di sky!
Si to it dat yout' don't die
Dry di eye of Black man cry

RASTA TIME NOW!
All yout' eye
On I NOW
To go forward.

Year 1972, St. Catherine, Jamaica

A LOVE THAT DIED

A Poem for My Nephew Robert (i)

The ring of the phone
Late that night in Santa Barbara town
My brown fright

Fay, is that Fay?
Robert died today.
He complained of a headache
Sonia took him to the hospital

A regular routine in his condition
She waited and waited
He sank very fast

When he died they stuck him
He had no blood to meet
The fight for life

Just a little brown blood
Trickled from his vein
And his eyes
His so-so eyes
Were still.

A Poem for My Nephew Robert (ii)

So-so eyes, in thin yellow face
Wondering at your pain
Can you take Robert to the
Hospital again?

Joints swollen, nurses rough
Why can't a five year old be tough?
Your cousin Ashley, reading storybooks

We refused to change the rhythm of our
Lives for you
Tomorrow, I'll take you for a ride
Tomorrow, tomorrow
Another day Robert

So-so eyes, hear my cries
From the darkness where you fled
Your sick bed
Vain pain, sickle cell anemia crises
Sucking your red blood
Robert, Robert, Shobert

Year 1971, Santa Barbara, California

Let me Lay you to Rest

Let me lay you to rest
In the shroud of our friendship
You, a gentile who never knew
What I did as a Black Jew

Let me lay you to rest
In the shroud of our friendship
You, who were crucified
On the altar of intellectual conceit.

Year 1991, Washington DC

Your Wedding Shroud

Your mother said all the women
Who loved you wept at your wedding
Such weeping and moaning
On the land she said

It was as if they knew beforehand
And were rehearsing your funeral
For your wedding suit became your shroud

Year 1991, Washington DC

A Ghost of the Past

I saw you smiling
A ghost of the past
Returning to haunt me
Resurrecting memories long dead

I saw you smiling
That endearing toothy grin
That always touched my heart
Felt the turning and twisting
The yearning springing new life

Our eyes met - yours requesting
Pulling me back to the life I had fled
I hesitated, time stood suspended
In the tropic air
Moist with promises
Enticing me back to the life I had fled

You spoke
Breaking decades of silence
With beckoning voice
I took a step toward you

"Hail Sistah"

The voice broke in arresting my journey

My guardian angel in flesh

Oblivious of the role he had played

I turned my back on you

Leaving forever

The life I once led.

Year 1992, Washington DC

Immortality through Death

Turning the pages of the Jamaican paper
Absent-mindedly
Your face darted from it
Startling me.

There you were, quite dead
The news clip said

But instead
You sprang to life from the place
I had buried you

Opening floodgates of youthful memories
Flowing within me
Ensuring your immortality
by dying

Year 1992, Washington DC

Parting was such Sweet Sorrow

Parting was such sweet sorrow
I steeled myself with the trembling joy of it
For I was raised a Roman Catholic
And loved my bleeding heart

Parting was such sweet sorrow
I gloried in its pain
I wasn't thinking of tomorrow
Only the ecstasy of my sorrow

But when your voice became
Eternally still
Reality checked in.

Year 1992, Washington DC

Death and Resurrection

The rain washed down
On brown
Earth

They announced
The USSR died
And pronounced your death too

You and It fell apart
Same time
The earth cried
And Africa revived

March 2014, Paul Laurence Dunbar Apts., Washington DC

IN SEARCH OF BETTA MUST COME IN FOREIGN LANDS

Air Jamaica

We are the Jewmaycans

We Jamaicans are the wandering Jews of creation
We are loved and despised by many nations
We travel over hills and oceans
Face ice and snow
There is no place we won't go
To better our situation

We survive and thrive
Where others would drop dead
Oppose us and you know our worth
As our great Marcus Garvey said

We light the fire that set things in motion
We provide the spark that erupts into revolutions
Look at what Boukman did for Haitians
And you will understand our notion

We are the wandering Jews of creation
We are the Jewmaycans!

Year 2012, Paul Laurence Dunbar Apts., Washington DC

She Wanted to Know

But she wanted to know other worlds
Other worlds   outside
her island world
Worlds of ice and snow
Worlds where tropic winds did not blow

She wanted to know other worlds
She loved Jamaica, yes
With its Poinciana trees blooming
Red flowers waving against sun-strained skies
In the summer
And the poinsettias
rustling flame-like in Christmas breezes

The misty mountains, green hills
Shiny jeweled seas and creamy sands
Far away from the white world of America

Yet she wanted to know other worlds
Worlds of ice and snow
Worlds where the tropic winds did not blow

Worlds of progress and mobility

Worlds where with determination

One could make it to the top

Worlds with large skies

So unlike the limited skies of Jamaica

She wanted to know other worlds

She wanted

To know.

Year 1972, Green Hills, Portland, Jamaica

Dem Old-time West Indians

Dem old-time West Indians
Liked to talk about how they too
Fought in the Black revolution
Right beside Black Americans

Some a dem march with Martin Luther King
Some leggq dem mowt pon racists white man
Some shout out loud how dem black an' proud
An' put up big fight fi dem rights

Plenty a dem force white people to behave
An' show dem dat dem is no slave
An' set good example to Black people in America
By refusing to mek white people cow dem

If it was egg, dem was in di red
an if it was fish, dem was di buttah
Dem was neck an' neck fi di fight
Fi dem 'uman rights an' civil action to Black people

(ii)

In dem days wi use to carry British passport
For wi was British colonies, not independent like now
Some a wi tek wi passport so bruck dung race barriers
Flashing it ina segregationist face
So wi cyahn go inna any place
even if it mark white only

For as loyal British subject wi was unda British protection
An' though Britain treat wi bad, shi tink is shi alone to do it
An' like mek up hypocrite noise when America faas wid wi

Wi action strengthen Black 'Merican
An' help dem say yes wi cyahn
For if we foreign Negroes cyahn
An' dem is citizen, dem cyahn to

Is not jus' di famous Caribbean ones like Marcus Garvey
and Belafonte who help the Black struggle
Wi di people pon di ground was a-mek history too'
Is time dem write fi wi story.

Year 2012, Bath, St. Thomas, Jamaica

The Uprooted One

So here I am
The uprooted one
Existing precariously
Between
Caribbean nationality
America
Africa and Europe
Integrated in none

(ii)
Trying ever so often to run back to my island
Only to face the reality of no turning back
My island paradise rejects me
Except
As an overseas one bringing gifts
For their long lists
I have lost my place.

The 1990's, Washington DC

Lost Angels

Caribbean immigrants who go to foreign lands

Seeking security, fame, success

Try their best to pass the test as achievers

They can't let people back home know they're flops

Excluded from cliques that have made it

Who can return laden with foreign goods

And send barrels with gifts

Basking in the approval of islanders

who live vicarious foreign lives

Through the things from faraway places over seas

Those Caribbean immigrants

With shattered dreams gasping for life

Those who no one remembers

When boasting of our successes

Those walking the streets of America, Canada and Europe

Longing for warm childhood

Innocence lost

Unable to go home

The 1990's, Washington DC

Here We Are

Here we are in America
Marooned from islands that once encircled us
And were the only world we knew

Here we are with our decision
Trying to fulfill our vision
That led us to leave our islands

Here we are in the cold hands of immigration
Oblivious of the weight of our separation
And the raging waters of our pain

Our attempts to gain sympathy are in vain
They have no empathy for our situation
And don't care about our tears
Or ruptured affairs
Created by the landscape of our absence

While we try to satisfy
Claims they require for reunions
Here we are.

Year 2012, Paul Laurence Dunbar Apts., Washington DC

It was on Those Nights

On weekends those of us in foreign
Gathered to talk about the homeland
On summer nights we endured
New York's heat with whirling fans
And thought of cooling Trade Winds of our islands

On winter nights they turned up the heat to 80f. or higher
And used the warmth and glow of Appleton white or red
Their laughter's brightness contrasting winter's gloom

(ii)
It was on those nights that as a young girl
I learned of the 1938 riots that ripped my island
And broke the heart of Jamaica's white governor,
poor thing

And made England send to find out
What the hell was going on in her loyal colony
And offer us Adult Suffrage to cool independence fires

(iii)

It was on those nights

Those overseas Caribbean gathering nights

That I was force-fed slavery's realty

And learned to embrace ancestors from Africa

As kith and kin ancestral

Blood relatives who suffered slavery

So that I could be

(iv)

It was on those nights

Those summer nights

Those winter nights

That I learned to love our folk songs

And comprehend my island.

Year 2012, Bath, St. Thomas, Jamaica

Memories of Warm Decembers

When Christmas breeze blows in my island
When sorrel is drank with rum
When Christmas comes in the sun

Oh how my heart sinks to my feet
Dragging through these wintry streets
Cursing White Christmas

Tropic beats fill my ears
Locking out silver bells
Frozen tears spring to my cheek
Frozen dreams rests on my heart

Year 2007, South Dakota Ave, Washington DC

Sun Dreams in Wintry Lands

Enveloped in summer sun's embrace
Youthful dreams dance before my eyes
Days when I was young
And my world limited by Caribbean seas
And glistening white sands

I become forgetful of ravaging winter
in the metropolis where I am
remembering only eternal summerland
until summer withdraws her embrace
Autumn comes and bids farewell.

I am jolted to where I am
Huddling in frozen wintry worlds
I join the chorus
Sighing for warm homelands
Left behind in search of unfulfilled dreams
In foreign lands

Year 2007, South Dakota Ave, Washington DC

The Island of Our Love

My love is majestic mountains
Happiness refreshing the waterfall of my heart
Heartbreak of separation from the island of you

Longing for your cooling moist winds
And my face in your sun
Shimmering seas dancing with reflections
of your smile

Moonlit palm trees haunting me
Tropical memories whispering
As I walk cold Northern shores

The 1990's, Washington DC

Abeng-Binghi di Rasta Maroon

Hunted down by today's
slavemasters and their faithful serfs
Tracked for rebelling against treaty laws that impair
My right to infuse my redemption songs
down in Jamaica land

Tricked by the Promised peace
shipped out to foreign shores
to waterdown my fire or die

From exile I cry
for Repatriation to my
Afrikan homeland

Year 1991, Washington DC

Immigrant Mother Letter to Son

So many years of separation from you
So many fears
As you go you go through rites of passage

While I reside
in the land of Betta Mus' Come
the land of your dreams
You have joined the ranks of barrel children

Waiting for mother to send for them
Using barrel goods as comfort
For lack of her presence

Jah be with you my chile
Take this wish from me while
I live in exile
Across the seas

The 1990's, Washington DC

HAIL JAH RASTAFARI

Nyabinghi Gathering, Jamaica

I-Lan' in di Sun

Jah mek yah
I land in di sun
Green trees
cool breeze
Washing rivas of I blood
Four 'undred years flood

Jamaica
Earth shakah
Earthquakah
Babylon maykah
Babylon breakah

I voice cry within thee
Incessantly
Set I free
From uncertainty
Sen' I home
Let I roam
I true land
Africa

The 1970's, Green Hills, Portland, Jamaica

(ii)

Jamaica

Rock of Resistance

Blessed and cursed land

Thou who must sink

Undah waata

Afta di terrible slawtah

Pit of Jehoshaphat

To which all nations must come

Fear not

For thou was chosen to birth

The prophet Marcus Garvey

The Black Star

The rising of sons and daughters

Of The Most High

Rastafari

I and I

The 1970's, Green Hills, Portland, Jamaica.

Christ, the Rastaman

I meet Christ dreadlocked
In rain soaked island mountains
Cooking Ital stew
Reasoning with man and man
While Mary listens
And Martha fusses at household tasks

Christ is the righteous Rastaman
Walking by the Caribbean Sea
Just as he did in Galilee

Christ yods our hills and valleys
And heat waved ghetto streets
Wearing sampatas
In the temple of a Rastaman

Christ is alive and well in man
He is a righteous African
I see H.I.M. in the bible
Especially John
Christ steps from its pages
And becomes, a Rastaman

Christ is risen in the Rastaman!

I read it in Revelation frequently

This makes the word incarnate in me

And the bible no longer a mystery

Or the fulfilMANt of prophecy

I face the future with tranquility

Illuminated by Jeremiah 31:3; Ps. 43:8; Heb 16:15-18

Luke 10:42-48; Mark 4:14-23

Year 1994, Tuckerman St., Washington DC

Di Road to Mt. Zion

Di road narra an' steep, I sistren
Di road to damnation
Is a broad, smooth road
But di road to Mt. Zion
Is a narra narra road
Is a steep steep road
Dat lang an' tilesome

Di road narra an' steep, I sistren
It blista di foot
It tes' di spirit
For Satan done know 'im lose
But outa spite 'im a-try di patience
of I an' I, Jah righteous saints

Di jerney lang an' 'ard, I sistren
Di jerney to Satan is a easy easy wan
But di jerney to Mt. Zion, it lang an' wearsome
Yet I'll neva tun back, though di fire be hot
I shall not, shall not leave
Di lang an' tilesome road, to Mt. Zion

Year 1970, Green Hills, Portland, Jamaica

Rainbows of The Promised Land

She sings her blues in the ghettos
Empty refrigerator
Money dunny – no cash
Everyting a-crash
Trials and tribulation pon the poor of di lan'

She sings that one day she will overcome
And fly over rainbows in the Promised Land
She croons to her baby son
And lives in hope he will grow up to be a strong man
And escape the stranglehold of Babylon

She sings of rainbows of the Promised Land
And dreams of horizons she'll fly beyond
When she goes forward to Ethiopia land
Bye and bye.

Year 2009, South Dakota Avenue, Washington DC

A Living Sacrifice

Battering from pillar to post
No food to eat
No place to sleep
Pointed guns
As my daily bread

Battering from pillar to post
Like the son of man
Foxes have holes
Birds have nests
But I have no place to rest

From pillar to post
I offer up myself
As a living sacrifice of love.

Illuminated by Is. 54:17; Is. 66:5-7

Year 1975, Duhaney Park, Jamaica.

The Rastafari Queen

Queen Omega rules the night
While her Kingman the sun rules the day
She is the Mother of all
Who is not at all like weak willed Eve

Queen Omega, the Mother of Iration
Keep the irey vibration
For I and I liberation

She rules the night with irey moonlight
Soft and mellow, silver and yellow
Magical and wondrous is her light

A reflection of the sun
Since time begun
Yet different for sure
Is her method to conjure
Though she draws her strength
From the male sun

Queen Omega, the ila moon Queen

The Rastafari Queen

Her Kingman, the sun

Her children - the stars.

Year 1980, East Palo Alto, California

Call I Sistah Love

I am Sistah Love
The womb from which Rastafari spring
One Perfect Love is the key I bring
Malice, backbiting,
Backstabbing gwey
Of love I sing

Call I Sistah Love
Sistah Love is I name
I am a Rasta woman
I don't play games

Call I Sistah Love
Sistah Love is I name
That Love name
I now reclaim

Give it forward to me
Let I true worth be found
Let I name now resound
Call I Sistah Love
Crown I wid love

Year 2007, South Dakota Ave, Washington DC

Woman Clothed With The Sun

Woman clothed with the sun
Who knows how the race is won
Woman clothed with the sun
The son of Jah

Woman clothed with the sun
Giving Ises to the Almighty One
Prophetess, Queen
Friend of Jah
Woman clothed with the sun
Oh Rastafari Woman.

Year 1984, Santa Monica, California

I and I Children are I Stars

I and I children are I stars
The makers of the Iyatas
Into the Mothers of Iration

I and I children must be
Like the sand upon the sea
I and I line gone out into the heavens
Iternally

Year 1980, East Palo Alto, California

Synopsis of Birth and Growth of Rastafari

Coming in with showers breaking drought
Male child born in Harar, Ethiopia
First to survive, not die like other siblings
Immortal Rastafari rise to King
Relative of King Solomon
Colonial Afrikans sing

Emperor's coronation as Haile Selassie I
Celebrated worldwide
Opening Afrikan eyes
Afrika awakened as Marcus Garvey prophesied

Inspiring humble ones in Jamaica to organize
Rainbow love to end downpression
Teach reality that with righteousness
Victory certain

Caribbean leaders hell bent
To stomp out the new religion
With better dead than dread decisions
Bob Marley, reggae music, fly free
Rainbow visions shine internationally

Year 2009, South Dakota Ave, Washington DC

WRITING MY SOUL

In the Blue Mountains

The Softness in Our Lives

The softness in our lives
Hidden under layers of protective crusts
yearns to be free
And touched tenderly
So it can live

To strengthen us
Against hurts preceding inspirations
That carry us to levels we must achieve
In order to perceive

How to rise
And receive
The New Day

Year 1992, Washington DC

I Am Ready

With open heart
And outstretched hands
I stand
Receiving the fire's warming of my soul

It's cleansing of my inner me
I will go forward
Fire encircling my bowels
Billowing my imagination
Burning out negative vibrations
Opening me up to creation

Leading me on
To my destination
I am ready
To move
On

Year 2012, Paul Laurence Dunbar Apts., Washington DC

Writing my Soul (i)

The sound of sea shells

Lull me

Into serene afternoons of my childhood

Speaking to me softly

Through time's language

In the silent solitude of blooming flowers

I hear voices rising in towering

Island mountains

Whispering against my skies

Waving

The flag of my heart

Year 2012, Paul Laurence Dunbar Apts., Washington DC

Writing my Soul (ii)

I love to write in solitude

Blissfully listening to pen

Inking paper

Words pouring

From me

Like rain

Into parched earth

My pen/pencil

Gliding

Sliding

Storming rain words

Breaking the long drought

The 1990's, Washington DC

Writing my Soul (iii)

Sitting in a corner

As a large eyed child

Trying to unravel meaning from my world

Patiently putting its puzzle pieces in place

One window

Was all I needed to explore

Warm my insides with

Word sunshine

Pouring from the inner crevices of my being

One window was all

I needed in childhood

To solve my world

And need now

To write my soul

Year 2009, South Dakota Ave., Washington DC

Rising on Hope

Massaged by hope
I rise from the threshold of sorrow
On the wings of the faithful
I rise

In the incense
Of ascending prayer
Freshly renewed

I rise
I rise

Year 2000, Havendale, St. Andrew, Jamaica

I Am That I Am

I am

That I am

What I am

Free spirit

Unbowed

by tribulation

Staying true

To my vision

Imparting

My wisdom

A griot in the west.

The 1990's, Washington DC

I Shall Arise

I shall arise in the morning
I shall witness the dawning of a new day for Afrika
I shall arise in the morning to the sound of the drums
I shall come Mother Afrika
I shall come
I shall come.

Year 1970, Green Hills, Portland, Jamaica.

Glossary

Please note that the spelling of many words ending in *er* are changed to *a* or *ah,* and those ending with *ing* are changed to *in'* to give a better idea of their pronunciation in patois.

A

a-axe	. is asking
Abeng	A musical instrument made of a cows horn, brought to Jamaica by the Akan people of Ghana in the 1600's, used to communicate and celebrate by the Maroons in war and peace.
afta	after
agen	again
ah	I, a
ahr	her
ahrself	herself
'air	hair
Ananse	The storyteller-hero-trickster spider (assistant to the Sky God) from West Africa who came to the Caribbean in the memories of enslaved Africans.
Ankcestors	ancestors
apposite	opposite
'ave	have
axe	ask

B

Binghi	Shortened version of Nyahbinghi, a Rastafari way of life promoting the conquest of good over evil by restoring the unity of the creation with the Creator and Africans to their spiritual heights. Their traditional praise chanting and drumming is also called Nyahbinghi/Binghi.
blista	blister
bout	about
bredda	brother
browning	light-skinned black woman
bruk	break/broke, bruk pocket - no money
Brutish	British
Brutan	Britain
bus'	burst

C

caahn	can't
cahr	car
cawf	cough
chile	child
chileood	childhood
cloze	Clothes
cow dem	make them cower
cyahn	can

D

dat	That
ded	dead
dem	them
di	the
dose	those
downpression	oppression
dred	dreadlocks
dung	down
dunny	Money (because it is soon done)

E

eena	into
'ed	head
'eding	heading
everyting	Everything

F

faas'	fast, critical, inquisitive/curious, nosy, fast living
fi	for
fulfilMANt	fulfillment
fus	first

G

gaan	gone
gi	give
gwaan	go on
gwey	go away
gwine do	going to do
gyal	girl

H

haffi	have to
heducation	education

I

'ide	hide
ila	good, alright
'im	him
inspecta	Inspector. A title of a high ranking policeman.
iration	Jah creation, the world/universe
irey, irie	It is good, in divine order, alright
i-lan', i-lant	island
Ithiopia	Ethiopia
Iyata	Daughter of Jah. A title of a Rastafari woman.

J

Jahmekyah	Jah make here/Jah made here. A Rastafari name for Jamaica.
jerney	journey
Jewmaycan	Jew maker. Nickname that African Americans used to give to Jamaicans in New York because of their thriftiness and love of purchasing property.

K

kip	keep
Kingman, King	The title of a Rastafari male, how a Rastafari female (Queen) refers to her male counterpart.

L

lan'	land
lang	long
larn	learn
leggo	let go
lissen	listen

M

Maroons	Africans and their descendants who refused to be enslaved and formed their own communities in inaccessible terrain. In Jamaica, they fought the British for eighty-three years until the British sued for peace through a treaty.
mawnin'	morning
mek	make
'Merican	American
mine'	mind
mowt	mouth

N

nah	not
Nanni	Jamaican Maroon heroine's African name, meaning Great Queen Mother. The English spell her name Nanny.
narra	narrow
Nayga	Negro
neva	never
nise	noise
nobady	nobody
noh	don't, no
Nyahbinghi	see Binghi

O

offisah	police officer
ole	old
'oman	woman
ongly	only
outa	out of
ova	over
ow'	how

P

peeni walli	candle flies, fireflies
pickney	child
pitcher	picture
pon	upon

R

Rastafari	One who follows the philosophy of Emperor Haile Selassie I, whose name was Ras Tafari before his coronation.
ridah, rida	rider. Ridah dem means riders.
rivas	rivers
'roun	around
roun'	round
'rung	around

S

sah	sir
Sampatas	A sandal worn by early Rastafari people. It was first manufactured in Pinnacle, the first Rastafari commune. The soles of the sandals were made from car tires.
sarra	sorrow
seh	say
shi	she
si	see
silva	silver, make silvery
sinting	something
Sistah	sister
Sistren	sisters
slawtah	slaughter
smady	somebody
soljah	soldier
splutta	splutter
stap	stop

T

tanks, tank yu	thanks
tes'	test
tek	take
tiday	today
tigah	tiger
ting	thing
tings	things
tilesome	toilsome
tink	think
tomarra	tomorrow
trow	throw
tru	through
trubble	trouble
tuff	tough
tun	turn
tung	town

U

undah	under

W

waan	want
waata	water
wat	what
wen	when
wey	that, what
wi	we
wid	with
widout	without
wile	wild
wite	white
woulda	would have
wuk	work
wutless	worthless

Y

ya, yah	here
yesiday	yesterday
yeye	eye
yods	trods, go on a journey, walk
Yoyo	Maroon name for the children (people) of Maroon heroine Nanni.
yunda	thunder

Z

Zion wires	Mental telepath

About The Author

Nana Farika Fayola Berhane is a writer and cultural activist who was born in Kingston, Jamaica. She is the winner of medals in the genres of poetry, short fiction, children's stories and plays from the *Jamaica Cultural Development Commission, Black Writers contests,* and several grants for her arts education projects.

The Smithsonian Institution commended her officially *"in appreciation of exceptional contributions to the increase and diffusion of knowledge..,"* for her work with the Maroon people. *The Jamaican National Association* recognized her for *"excellence in Literary Arts,"* for the 50th Anniversary of Jamaica's independence.

Her work is published in Jamaica, London, Europe, and the United States. She was trained at the *London School of Journalism.* She studied creative writing at the *Instituto de Allende, Mexico* and the *Creative Writing Centre* of the *University of* the *West Indies,* playwriting at the *Circle in the Square Theater School* in New York, and scriptwriting with the *BBC.* She wrote scripts for *Jamaican Information Service* radio/television/film and for *Jamaica Broadcasting Corporation Television.*

Contact her at *queenomegacommunications@gmail.com*

I-LAN' IN DI SUN